THE CALL
of the
MOURNING
DOVES

Meeting God in Reality

MARY KATHY GRAY

CITI OF
BOOKS

CITIOFBOOKS, INC.
3736 Eubank NE Suite A1
Albuquerque, NM 871113579
www.citiofbooks.com
Hotline: 1 (877) 3892759
Fax: 1 (505) 9307244

Ordering Information:

Quantity sales. Special discounts are available on quantity purchases by corporations, associations, and others. For details, contact the publisher at the address above.

Printed in the United States of America.

ISBN13:	Softcover	979-8-89391-314-9
	eBook	979-8-89391-315-6

Library of Congress Control Number: 2024920671

The Call of the Mourning Doves

A Collection of Inspirational Prayers

Especially for

_____

(Name)

With Love and Affection from

_____

(Name)

On

_____

(Date)

TABLE OF CONTENTS

SPECIAL THANKS

To my mother

Marja Lee Dalton Hoffman

June 11, 1928–November 18, 2016

To my mother for her undying affection, support, and belief in my call to write for our Lord Jesus Christ. Her encouragement was my constant. She once wrote to me, "Received your writings today and read all of it. I was moved by what I read and thank God that you have had the courage to pursue your heart's desire and pray the Lord's blessing and anointing on your life. It is my prayer that the writings will bless others and change their lives to have the desire to come to know the Lord and serve Him." Mother, thank you for being a constant in my life, helping me to remain focused on the God of my heart. Thank you for your support through the valleys of my life and for your encouragement to rise up and walk in the light of the Lord.

PREFACE:
THE CALL OF THE
MOURNING DOVES

Be still, and know that I am *God.*

—Psalm 46:10

D awn is breaking—the first light as the softness of early morning, gray-blue skies evolve from the darkness. A single star shining brilliantly in a clear sky will soon disappear into the depths of the heavens as gray-blue fades into the whiteness of the day.

The air, moist and cool, awakens the birds, ushering them into flight to see which one can get to the first meal of the day, each trying to outdo the other. Squawking, crowing, and shrieking fill the air as they compete for the bounty beneath them.

As my footsteps take me deeper into the woods, I become aware of the greatness of our Creator. Water seeping from within the rocks, filling the earthen trough with cool, clean, bubbling refreshment, quenches my thirst and replenishes my body with life-giving fluid. Absorbing the mysteries of a simple leaf, a rock along the path, and a fossilized urchin hiding in the gravel of the creek bed, I come to realize how small I am in the scheme of things. As God's greatness evolves about me,

I see how meticulously He planned, how every creation from miniscule to massive supports life, each for the other.

As I walk amid His greatness, I come to realize I am no greater than a grain of sand beneath my feet and no smaller than the mightiest of all His creations. Simply put, *I am* because of Him! I live and breathe, not of my own will but simply because He allows it. My heart races, and my breath catches me. "Be still, and know that I *am* God" (Psalm 46:10).

As dawn breaks into brilliant sunlight, I hear the call of the mourning doves—coo, coo, coo—reminding me that as I live in Christ Jesus, walking in His stead, He surely has never left me or forsaken me. He is neither behind me nor in front of me. His steps are synchronous with mine; He walks beside me. I envision His hand holding mine, warm and comforting, as I tell Him the desires of my heart. I see Him smile with approval as I sing praises to Him. I hear His mellow voice telling me as I lay my sins before Him, "Be strong and of a good courage, fear not, nor be afraid of them: for the Lord thy God, He it is that doth go with thee; He will not fail thee, nor forsake thee" (Deut. 31:6). I am drawn to His soothing tones that fill me with confidence and bolster my belief. As my heart is cleansed and I am filled with His Spirit, the earth, wet with dew, seems to glow with freshness of life renewed. Then ever so faintly, far in the distance, I hear the soft cooing of the mourning doves. My heart surges with renewed strength. I smile as I listen, my soul resting peacefully and extraordinarily calm as God speaks to my heart through the call of the mourning doves.

—Mary Kathy Gray

FOREWORD

I was born into poverty in 1949 and lived in government projects for the first three years of my life. I can still see in my mind's eye the ugly gray color of the walls. I can still feel the cold, hard concrete underneath my feet. The memory of cold air in the apartment still makes me shudder.

My mother was 21 years old when I was born. She worked as a waitress, barely making ends meet to take care of my two brothers and me. My father worked in trucking, transporting cattle from one state to another. I rarely saw him, and when he was home, he gave us children little attention. He became ill and passed from this life to the next life at age 33. Mother was destitute, alone with three children and very lonely. She was deeply saddened, and life became very difficult for us all. I think we felt her sadness, as young as we all were.

About a year later, she began dating a man. She prayed to God to bring her a husband who could not only love her but take on the responsibility of her three children and love them as his own. She married this man, and he was a wonderful husband and father, kept a good job, and took care of all of us.

Born Again

I was raised in church and was saved when I was 16 years old, but I did not have a spiritual relationship with God until January 6, 1986, when I experienced a Damascus Road meeting with Jesus Christ who delivered me from the bonds of Satan and set me free. It was as if I had been on a very long journey and was returning home. With my eyes filled with tears, I prayed, "Jesus, bring me home." Instantly, I was delivered from the bonds of Satan. I had been lost, but now I was found.

Since that date, God has been ever present with me as I have walked through the trials of hatred and jealousy among friends; the valleys of death at the loss of loved ones; and fears for myself, my husband, and my children at the loss of jobs and living in low economic surroundings.

My desire to commune with God and feel His actual presence with me was so strong that I wanted and needed a place to meet with Him, a place of solace and peace. It had to be a place where I could sing my heart out to Him in praise. I found such a place as I walked along woodland trails and talked with Him at the break of dawn, being kissed by Him as the sun's rays broke through the clouds.

He was there when my twin sons were born much too early and when one of them failed to survive the birth. It was His strength that kept me awake around the clock to keep my remaining son alive. Then He blessed me with a third son and then a fourth son who could not survive a premature birth. Yes, four sons—two alive—and I am blessed. But the pain of loss is great.

"Not my will but Thy will," I prayed, relinquishing my eldest son to him as he lay near death with a fatal disease. "He's your son. I give him to you, O God." Then suddenly he is healed of the disease that has no known cure.

God was there while I cried on His shoulder when my 32-year marriage was breaking apart and breaking my heart. Betrayal and threat of death from a much loved and trusted family member brought me emotional pain and shock. Tears flowed like rain. I was filled with anger. God was there and protected me from this evil person driven by greed. God helped me forgive this individual, but the broken trust between us could never be restored.

What about my bad choices? Even then I felt God's arm around my shoulders as I cried out in anger at my own stupid mistakes, chastising myself for my inept mind, crazy with fear when I did not know which way to turn and not realizing He was holding my hand and guiding me through dark shadows as I ran blindly, trying to figure life out. He held me in the palm of His hand, whispering in my ear, "I got this. Just trust Me."

God would show me how much I would suffer for His sake during a heart procedure in which I began screaming at the top of my lungs from unbearable pain. Now I am alive and can continue working under His call of many years ago to write for Him to show the world He is real, and His Word is true.

There have been lessons taught, lessons learned, and blessings untold by understanding and revelation from the I AM. He chose me before I could choose Him.

He has chosen *you*! Take this journey, and enjoy the soft cooing of the doves that assure you that peace is coming to your life and that God is waiting for you to come into relationship with Him.

chapter 1

ABOUT PRAYER

Jesus Christ's purpose in coming to earth was to make known the difference in our level of existence and His level of existence, and to help us understand the triune God the Father, Jesus the Son, and the Holy Spirit. He also came to teach us how to reach His level by way of Spirit connection and in doing so bring forth cleanliness of the heart and subsequent salvation from our fleshly sins. As we seek to make this Spirit connection, we must be willing to give up those desires that bind us to Satan's power in our flesh. We must want this connection more than we want life itself. We must be ready to submit to the will of the Father and desire change in our circumstances, effecting a change of heart. Subsequently, our values and priorities will change. Once we have *sincerely* approached God to connect spiritually, the sin will burst forth from our hearts, cleansing us by His grace, His compassion, and His suffering on the cross. The sin will be replaced with the Spirit of God filling us and anointing us to receive His gift of communion with Him. You will know you have been visited by the Lord for "behold, the kingdom of God is within you" (Luke 17:21). God wants to commune with us daily; however, it is because of our unbelief that we do not attempt to move into that higher plane that reaches Him on His communal level—a choice that denies His power to resolve issues that plague our carnal being.

We must acknowledge the superiority and authority of our spiritual Father God by and through prayer in which we can communicate to Him and with Him the innermost desires of our hearts. It is when we acknowledge our inability to deliver ourselves from the bonds of Satan, as well as our lack of perfection within ourselves, that we come to understand God and what He wants for our lives.

In seeking out the Lord God, we must always approach Him in prayer, by and through the Holy Spirit, our Comforter, who will petition God on our behalf to approach His throne. As Jesus admonished the disciples, "After this manner therefore pray ye: Our Father which art in heaven, Hallowed be thy name. Thy kingdom come. Thy will be done in earth, as it is in heaven. Give us this day our daily bread. And forgive us our debts, as we forgive our debtors. And lead us not into temptation, but deliver us from evil: For thine is the kingdom, and the power, and the glory, forever. Amen" (Matthew 9:1–13). There is amazing power in the Lord's Prayer since it calls the Holy Spirit into power in our hearts and opens the doors of communion with the Father.

As we approach the Father through prayer, Jesus instructs us to pray without an audience. "And when thou prayest, thou shalt not be as the hypocrites are: for they love to pray standing in the synagogues and in the corners of the streets, that they may be seen of men. Verily I say unto you, they have their reward" (Matthew 6:5). As a child, I remember seeing a preacher standing on a street corner in the city, shouting biblical scripture and praying as people walked by. People were looking at him as if he was a lunatic. No one was receiving the blessings that praying affords the believer because it was the wrong environment, the wrong place, and the wrong time. No doubt, this man believed he was called to share the good news with others, and perhaps he carried a great burden for lost souls; however, God is a *person* and wants a personal and intimate relationship with us through prayer with Him.

Think about the intimate relationships you have had in your life with family members and friends. Did you go out onto the street and shout to everyone your love and affection for that person? Of course not! To this day, we hold secrets of affection in our hearts that are special only to that person and you. This is what God wants as well. He wants to get inside us and allow us to get inside Him. He wants to be intimate with us, and the affections He displays to us are for our hearts only. No one else around us can receive what is special for us from God, and shouting from the streets or being obvious in a worship service does not lift us up to the communion plane. It only creates abhorrence and embarrassment to others who must endure our vain babblings. We do not have to shout from the rooftops to get recognition because God will meet our need for recognition through our trust and belief in Him for our emotional fulfillment.

Jesus never made Himself a spectacle while He communed with His Father. Even when He was with the disciples, He prayed in private and told them, "Sit ye here, while I go and pray yonder. And he went a little farther, and fell on his face, and prayed" (Matthew 26:36) within the secrecy of the Garden, He prayed to His Father God. "But thou, when thou prayest, enter into thy closet, and when thou hast shut thy door, pray to thy Father which is in secret; and thy Father which seeth in secret shall reward thee openly" (Matthew 6:6).

The word *closet* has many and various definitions. However, in the context of spirituality, it is defined as "a place of retreat or privacy: closet of the heart." It may be further defined as "a place of seclusion, study, or speculation." Another definition is "to take into a closet for a secret interview."

God was not in the habit of communing with people in public places. His first communion with people was in the privacy of the Garden of Eden that was bound and gated. God communed with people in the privacy "above the mercy seat" behind heavy curtains in the temple. He communed with Moses on a high mountain far above the people. Jesus retreated to the Garden of Gethsemane located high on a hill overlooking the city below. In all these instances, the important factor was privacy. When communing with people, God wants their undivided attention and complete consecration. God did not specify that we had to have a special place that was only used for prayer. He simply set the example that through privacy with Him, He would reward us openly. Reward comes in the knowledge that yes, there is God—one God who is Alpha, Omega, the first, the last, before the foundation of the world. Before Him there was no God formed, and neither shall there be after Him who is omnipresent, awesome with power, and magnificent in grace. He gives peace that passes all understanding and joy unspeakable.

Perhaps you have a special place you like to visit with God, but you cannot allow your failure to be at that place to hinder you from communing with God as you desire. We cannot allow ourselves to feel we must be in church in order to find God. He is constantly with us everywhere where we go. The secret is to build a "closet" around ourselves wherever we are. To draw imaginary walls around ourselves, we seek the Holy Spirit and deliver our praise and requests. Shut out to the world, and allow your spirit to flow into a higher plane. Reach for God on His level. Jesus said, "After this manner therefore pray ye, Our Father, who art in Heaven, hallowed it be thy name" (Matthew 6:9).

In Dr. John Maxwell's study book *One Hour with God*, he suggests waiting on the Lord to reveal His love for us and allow Him to search us for impurity and show us what we need to know about ourselves. Dr. Maxwell advocates confessing sin, interceding for others, petitioning for ourselves, praying the scriptures, becoming obedient, and believing. Finally, he says to praise Him for who He is and thank Him for what He has done in our lives.[1]

We should ask only once. "But when ye pray, use not vain repetitions, as the heathen do: for they think that they shall be heard for their much speaking. Be not ye therefore like unto them: for your Father knoweth what things ye have need of, before ye ask him" (Matthew 6:7).

We pray, *hoping* that God will hear us, not with *believing* and *expectation*. God wants us to not only believe with all that is within us but to also expect Him to answer our prayers and

---

1. John C. Maxwell, *One Hour with God*, Injoy, Inc., 1994.

fill our needs. When we rely solely on Him to grant our wishes and fulfill our needs, He knows that we truly do believe and that we expect Him to control what is good for our life. It is because we do not pray only *once* and relinquish our request to His control that we feel we must pray continually. We *hope* He will hear us and are disappointed and disillusioned when He does not answer our requests as we *hoped* He would. We must believe and receive: "If ye then, being evil, know how to give good gifts unto your children: how much more shall your heavenly Father give the Holy Spirit to them that ask him?" (Luke 11:13). Ask Him once *believing*, and then turn it over to Him—relinquish control. "Therefore I say unto you, what things so ever ye desire, when ye pray, believe that ye receive them, and ye shall have them" (Mark 11:24). "And all things, whatsoever ye shall ask in prayer, believing, ye shall receive" (Matthew 21:22).

It was devastating the day I learned that my eldest son had been stricken with a fatal disease at the young age of twenty-five. It was an incurable disease, and no one seemed to know what to do. It was not a cancer that could be treated with chemotherapy. It was a rare autoimmune disease called aplastic anemia that attacks healthy blood cells by attacking the stem cells in the bone marrow. Cells were being destroyed in my son's blood system as fast as they were being created, causing a huge shortage of blood cells in order for the body to operate. He was being given blood every day. I was his caretaker at home, and I watched his life ebbing away. I prayed a prayer that acknowledged God's right to take him home. I offered him up to God if He so chose to take him to heaven instead of healing him to spend a longer life with me. I read scripture in the book of John. "If ye abide in me, and my words abide in you, ye shall ask what ye will, and it shall be done unto you" (John 15:7). So I gave my son back to God if He wanted him. I held God's Word literally next to my heart. I told God that His choice would be okay with me since I knew He would get me through the grief over the loss of my son. At that very moment, God intervened and healed my son instantaneously!

The prayers of this book are about desire and intimacy with God. They are about the struggle to come into the reality of God. They are about choice—a choice to believe the reality of God and believe that He wants to commune with you.

These prayers take you to the core of your inner self and unlock the secrets of the heart. You will be exposed to the realization that the humanness of your being is created inept. You are incomplete without a personal relationship with Jesus your Savior, your Father God, and your Comforter His Holy Spirit. You are incomplete without personal communion with God. He desires it, and your life source—His Spirit within you—thrives on it. As you read this book, let the words of these prayers become the words of your heart to your Father. Read them, and pray them to your "daddy," Abba Father. Through these prayers, let Him hear the supplications of your true self. Cut away the facade you have created for the world, and let God enjoy your true being just as He created you. Share your innermost desires and thoughts that are not for human ears.

These prayers are to help you learn how to commune with the Lord on a spiritual plane that is above earthly rhetoric and self-reliance. This is a plane of submission on which you will become broken and molded by the hand of God. It is a plane of humbleness on which the essence of your being will cry out in anguish for deliverance from outstretched hands that demand your "life blood" that keeps you from intimacy with God. Let your mind flow from the earth into the heavens to elevate you to the plane of submissiveness and humbleness. On this plane, you will allow walls to fall and chains to be broken that have prevented you from operating as the being you were created to be—a holy and communicative entity energized by the power of the Holy Spirit to meet with God in reality. You will receive the peace and joy God intended for you.

chapter 2

PRAYER AND COMMUNION

In the beginning, God came down to earth to commune and have fellowship with His creation—humans. God's human creations were not born of fleshly bodies but were supernaturally formed into the persona of God Himself. Adam and Eve knew from their days in the Garden of Eden with God that He was their creator and Father. They looked to Him to provide their physical needs and protection. God gave Adam and Eve instructions for living in the Garden where they would forever visit and commune with Him daily. However, because Adam and Eve did not follow God's directions for living safely in the Garden, God was forced to separate Himself from them by driving them out of the Garden, a place of perfection.

Since that day of separation from God, people have yearned for communion with God the Father. From a very early age, humans have known they are incomplete unto themselves. Their greatest desire, conscious or unconscious, is to commune *directly* with God. The desire is unconscious because a person may not come into a conscious desire until they reach a serious need in a crisis that seems too big to handle on their own. Since we have been created for God's enjoyment and purpose, it is God's greatest desire to commune directly with us. His initial concept was that a person would enjoy a life of pleasure in surroundings that God would also enjoy—a place where He would visit that person and commune with them daily. Thus, God created Eden, which is from the Hebrew word that means "delight or a delightful place to walk and talk with His creation.

Consider that it is entirely possible to speak with and hear from God through a realistic encounter on a divine level. Scripture calls such an encounter "communion." To commune directly with the Father is truly divine. It is magnificent! God makes your purpose for being in this world crystal clear. You radiate God's love to all those you come in contact with. You bask in the sunlight of His love and mercy. The knowledge that you have come into the presence of the Father overwhelms you with joy. You have a magnetism that attracts people, and you sparkle with enthusiasm for life.

> *Yet have thou respect unto the prayer of thy servant, and to his supplication, O LORD my God, to hearken unto the cry and to the prayer, which thy servant prayeth before thee today.*
>
> —1 Kings 8:28

chapter 3

PRAYERS

And all things, whatsoever ye shall ask in prayer, believing, ye shall receive.

—Matthew 21:22

The Cross

A bloodstained cross dragging through a narrow street of stone,
The Via Dolorosa winding through ancient Jerusalem to the
place of persecution,
The place where the Christ died a savage death bearing the
sins of the world alone,
Crying out to the Father, "Forgive them, for they know not what they do."
For they do not comprehend the magnitude of the death of your Son.

A dark sky, wild and cold wind, lightning striking all around,
Three crosses silhouette against a blackened sky,
The earth quaking and groaning with anger,
People spitting, cursing, and laughing aloud,
As the Son of God is delivered unto death,
Giving birth to His kingdom, a kingdom of the Spirit
His Kingdom of a realm not comprehended by these men.

Blood dripping from slithers of flesh, thorns pricking pain to
the head of the King,
Tears streaming down His face, heartbroken, love embraced,
I beheld the King of kings hanging in my place.

By the grace of God, I stood at the foot of the cross,
I felt His pain and suffering and came to understand His loss.
His cross I gladly bear to continue His work down here,
Spreading the Word, teaching others about the Christ,
Teaching others, "I am the way, I am the truth, I am the Life!"

—From "The Foot of the Cross"
by Mary Kathy Gray

Have not I commanded thee? Be strong and of a good courage; be not afraid, neither be thou dismayed: for the LORD thy God is with thee whithersoever thou goest.

—Joshua 1:9

Father, Give Me Strength to Make the Right Choice

Father, You gave me free will to make my own choices. Life seems to offer many options, but in reality, there are really only two options from which to choose. Life's journey brings me to two roads, each one lined with trees. The road to my right is filled with trees heavy laden with beautiful flowers emitting the fragrance of allure. There are enticing globes, moist and shining; their fruit appears perfect, but they are bitter and dark within. Standing tall are shallow roots hidden beneath the soil of deceit; against strong winds they cannot stand. These trees are lust, pride, and sin. Off to my left are gnarled trees bent low to the ground, providing shelter from the storm. Sweet fruit feeds an empty soul; its seeds replenish, preserve, and defeat. God's heart within wounded and scarred walls overcomes struggles, wins battles, and preserves life to those who walk beneath. It's up to me—the choice that I make. Father, give me strength to make the right choice; no mistake can I make. The price is too dear; the loss of heaven is too great. Amen.

No man can serve two masters: for either he will hate the one, and love the other; or else he will hold to the one, and despise the other. Ye cannot serve God and mammon.

—Matthew 6:24

> *From that time forth began Jesus to show unto his disciples, how that he must go unto Jerusalem, and suffer many things of the elders and chief priests and scribes, and be killed, and be raised again the third day.*
>
> —Matthew 16:21

Amazing Love

O, Holy Jesus, how You suffered for us. You felt the sorrow of leaving those who did not understand, those who did not know You—the sorrow for many, many who would never know You. How alone You must have felt while going through Your trials and torment, knowing all the while that You must do this thing, that You could not pass the cup lest we die blemished with sin and without forgiveness. "Father, forgive them; for they know not what they do" (Luke 23:34), You said to the Father. And yes, we did not know the magnificence of Your love and understanding, Your compassion for our loss, Your complete understanding of our inability to perceive who You really were then and who You are today. Forgive us, O Lord, for our complete stupidity and lack of compassion for You as Your body was racked with pain, muscles torn, bones disjointed as the life drained from Your body. Forgive us, O Lord. Amen.

> *Then Pilate said unto them, Why, what evil hath he done? And they cried out the more exceedingly, Crucify him.*
>
> —Mark 15:14

Marvel not that I said unto thee, Ye must be born again.

—John 3:7

That I Should Be Changed and Born Again

Father, I come before You, seeking Your touch that I should be changed and born again as a new creature that is a reflection of You. As Your love fills me, I am made different as the old character disappears and Your love passes from me through the birth canal of light and life. I am born again, a creation of beauty and grace unmatched by earthly influence or contrived representations of spirituality—an aura of light, unexplainable sweetness, love radiating. I know I have been changed, that You have touched me in a special way I cannot explain. It's such simplicity. You touch, and I am changed. You touch, and I am healed. You touch, and I am set free! Amen.

Jesus answered, Verily, verily, I say unto thee, Except a man be born of water and of the Spirit, he cannot enter into the kingdom of God.

—John 3:5

But thou, O Lord, art a God full of compassion, and gracious, Long suffering, and plenteous in mercy and truth.

—Psalm 86:15

Bring Me Home

Dear Jesus, I have seen and felt Your compassion for me. It changed my life forever. I never want to forget when and how You pulled me from the pit of hell, how You reached down from Your heaven took hold of a filthy rag, shook it, and washed it clean. Your Spirit melding with mine in sublime ecstasy filled the room in which my pitiful and tormented soul cried out in anguish. Lost and lonely, destitute and void, I cried, "Bring me home." Weary and ready to give up, I released it all to You, risking Your rejection but trusting. As the enemy sneered and chided me to disbelieve, I cried out, "O God, deliver me; help me!" Your love enveloped me; Your blood covered me; Your broken body absorbed my pain. Light filled the room and penetrated my heart. Tears streaming with peace, sweet peace, and joy overflowing, the King reigns. Amen.

Unto the upright there ariseth light in the darkness: he is gracious, and full of compassion, and righteous.

—Psalm 112:4

I came not to call the righteous, but sinners to repentance.

—Luke 5:32

Unless I Die Daily to Self, I Cannot Know You, Lord

I read of a God of old who tried to bring the will of the people into Him through stern measures of death, and yet the people failed to repent. Pride and stubbornness prevailed, alienating them from mercy and deliverance. Pride pronounced that repentance would unveil weakness, admitting to a *need* that would require a power greater than their own to reconcile. God forbid that pride should blind me to my need to repent, for I am a sinner! Unless I die daily to self, I cannot receive love or wisdom; I cannot know You, Lord.

You breathed life into my body made of dust and gave me a will to make my own choices. It is I who chose to experience evil and wicked ways. It is I who chose the path I would walk in Your day. You gave me a Savior and a Comforter to help me, but I chose to look inside myself for the answers. I did not look to my source, my God, my Creator. I chose to stumble and fall, my strength ebbing away, dying spiritual death each step of the way. You gave me the Bible, your words, to guide me, but I was too proud to listen to You. I was too independent to realize I needed You. You loved me with all Your heart. You released me because You loved me, knowing like the dove that flew away but returned to Noah that one day I, too, would return to You. With head down, eyes streaming with tears, broken heart and life in disarray, I came to You for healing and to pray. Overwhelmed with compassion for me, You cleansed me and forgave me because You love me. Amen.

> *The Lord is not slack concerning his promise, as some men count slackness; but is longsuffering to us-ward, not willing that any should perish, but that all should come to repentance.*
>
> —2 Peter 3:9

Search me, O God, and know my heart: try me, and know my thoughts: And see if there be any wicked way in me, and lead me in the way everlasting.

—Psalm 139:23–24

Chastise Me, O God, That My Spirit May Be Stripped of Pride

Chastise me, O God, that my spirit may be stripped of pride. Bring my spirit into submission. Come into the chambers of my heart. Make known every transgression. Identify every lust of this flesh that plagues my spirit. Remove the cobwebs and dust of the effects of this carnal world that I must abide in before coming to Thee. Make known every truth. Open the eyes of my heart to the reality of You. Let the ears of my heart hear Your voice. Let me listen to hear Your desires for my life. Help me to realize that as Your creation, I am being molded by Your hands and fashioned into a vessel to contain the ointment that heals and waxes the spiritual ailments of humankind. Your intent is not to break me but to make me into Thy servant, O Lord. Help me to know and receive Your purpose for my life. Let me offer You every ounce of my energy, every portion of my strength that Your power may flow through Your Spirit that is within me to touch hearts and reveal truth and righteousness. Amen.

Shall not God search this out? for he knoweth the secrets of the heart.

—Psalm 44:21

If a man therefore purge himself from these, he shall be a vessel unto honour, sanctified, and meet for the master's use, and prepared unto every good work.

—2 Timothy 2:21

My Desire Is to Serve You, O Lord

Here I am, Lord, meeting with You in this barren place, this place of isolation where You have stripped me of pride and asked that I sacrifice everything for You. You said, "Follow me, and I will make you fishers of men" (Matthew 4:19), so I give my heart up to my career. "Follow me; and let the dead bury their dead" (Matthew 8:22), so I give up all my activities but that which You call me to do. You said, "If any man will come after me, let him deny himself, and take up his cross, and follow me" (Matthew 16:24), so I give my energy to Your work. You said, "Go and sell that thou hast, and give to the poor, and thou shalt have treasure in heaven: and come and follow me" (Matthew 19:21), so I will sell my goods to buy the treasure hidden in the chambers of Your heart. I want to bid my family farewell, but You said, "Follow me," so I leave them in Your care. I know Your voice, Lord, and like a magnet, I am drawn to Your soothing tones as I hear You call. My desire is to please You and respond in obedience. My desire is to serve You, O Lord. "I will follow thee whithersoever thou goest" (Matthew 8:19).

My sheep hear my voice, and I know them, and they follow me: And I give unto them eternal life; and they shall never perish. My Father, which gave them me, is greater than all; and no man is able to pluck them out of my Father's hand. I and my Father are one.

—John 10:27-30

Who hath wrought and done it, calling the generations from the beginning? I the LORD, the first, and with the last; I am he.

—Isaiah 41:4

Direct Me, O Lord, That I May Follow Your Lead to My Destiny

I recall those days in Egypt when Moses, your chosen Hebrew, rose up among the barbarians of the desert. The pride of Egypt, chosen to rule a people who were not *his* people, was exalted, respected, and held in high esteem. Educated and nurtured to become the leader of a nation, Moses was "mighty in words and in deeds" (Acts 7:22). But You, Lord, touched Moses's heart as you have touched mine, changing our lives forever. Thousands of years have passed, but You have not changed. You are the same now that You were then—absolutely sovereign. Moses's destiny—my destiny—is your destiny! The complexity of life overshadows the reality of simplicity. From the conception of the world to rapture into heaven, ancient lives, present lives, future lives, and You, God, become encircled, joined end to end, changed into one magnificent energy! Help me, Lord, to grasp the magnitude of Your plan. Direct me, O Lord, that I may follow Your lead to my destiny. Sweeping the trash of my life out the door, I abandon all desire of the flesh so my vision shall increase in clarity so I can seize the ultimate prize. Amen.

Know ye not that they which run in a race run all, but one receiveth the prize?
   So run, that ye may obtain.

—1 Corinthians 9:24

Joy in the Morning

Heaven's gates open wide to those who believe,
Coming into the joy of the Lord to receive His blessing,
They come to know life everlasting.

How magnificent His glory, white raiment aglow,
Perpetual light, pure energy, incredible power,
Our Savior stands ready to deliver his children
from the magnet of the world, the devourer.

Oh, for the joy of the Lord, that which you,
Satan, have no power to destroy,
He hears the cry and cares deeply for the tormented soul,
Taking away the pain of destruction, joy,
ecstatic joy resides in my soul.

From "O for the Joy of the Lord"
by Mary Kathy Gray

Therefore I take pleasure in infirmities, in re-proaches, in necessities, in persecutions, in dis-tresses for Christ's sake: for when I am weak, then am I strong.

—2 Corinthians 12:10

Deliver Me, O God, while There Is Still Time to Save Me

Am I so weak that I run hot and cold, Jesus? Where does my fickle heart come from? Can I not sacrifice even a little of myself for You? Can I not let go of the lusts that bind me? O God, where is my salvation? Where is my soul? Why am I so easily swayed? My spirit berated, my well of life-giving water becomes drained. Fool that I am, my heart weakens and waxes cold. Deliver me, O God, while there is still time to save me before I stand at Your throne waiting to hear Your approval, but Your eyes turn away from me saying, "I never knew you; depart from me" (Matthew 7:23). Amen.

But we had the sentence of death in ourselves that we should not trust in ourselves, but in God which raiseth the dead: Who delivered us from so great a death, and doth deliver: in whom we trust that he will yet deliver us.

—2 Corinthians 1:9–10

Then shall ye return, and discern between the righteous and the wicked, between him that serveth God and him that serveth Him not.

—Malachi 3:18

Lord, Help Me to Identify the Evil That Pervades My Spirit

Water runs down a hill, rolling, tumbling, and gaining momentum. Seeking its own level, it grows in volume until it becomes a wall of energy that is impossible to stop. It destroys everything in its path, and so it is with evil! Subtle and deceitful, it begins as a raindrop falling on untended soil hardened over time by neglect. Clouds overshadow God's light, pouring out polluted drops filled with acid that eats away the goodness of the heart. As evil entraps the soul unaware, the drop becomes a trickle, the trickle a river, and the river a raging wall that kills, steals, and destroys all hope of righteousness and purity. Lord, help me to identify the evil that pervades my spirit with creeping fingers that grip my heart and causes me to fall into sin. Give me the gift of discernment that I may recognize the lascivious character of evil as it reveals itself to me in my hour of weakness. Protect me, O Lord, from the hand of evil. Amen.

The fear of man bringeth a snare: but whoso putteth his trust in the LORD shall be safe.

—Proverbs 29:25

Look upon mine affliction and my pain; and forgive all my sins.

—Psalm 25:18

The Power of Pain Exalts You, O Lord

Dear Lord, sometimes I need to remember the words You gave me while I was in a valley of grief that overshadowed Your presence. "Jesus, where are You?" I wrote. I do not hear You. I do not feel You. My eyes are swollen from tears. A heart torn apart and withdrawn from You, I cry, dear Jesus, where are You? Desire and pleasures with You from the past have all but gone away as I seek and search. I cannot find the way. Grieving for loss, overshadowed with pain, I shed tears that drop like torrents of rain. Focus, purpose, and joy escape me, and I walk as a stranger in a desert with hot, tortured feet with no place to go, nothing to eat. Wounded and beaten, my soul is in shreds with no life, and nothing left to give. Belief, faith, love—these I search for, wandering the desert afar, searching for You, Jesus, and asking that once again You will fill my heart. The power of pain exalts You, O Lord, and sets You before me that my blind eyes are opened. My strength renewed; my vision becomes clear. With my purpose reviewed and focus restored, the bush of Moses burns brightly. Forty years of desolation and obscurity teaches the purpose of pain that can only be quenched in the fire of the burning bush. Help me, O Lord, to recognize that the pain of my emotions has purpose and serves to draw me closer to You while I am yet estranged.

Help me know that even when I am in a valley of grief, on a sea of turmoil, or in a hot dry desert, You are ever present and waiting to hear me say, "Here I am, Lord, that You may deliver me and use me." Amen.

> *And when the LORD saw that he turned aside to see, God called unto him out of the midst of the bush, and said, Moses, Moses. And he said, Here am I.*
>
> —Exodus 3:4

Be strong and of a good courage, fear not, nor be afraid of them: for the LORD thy God, he it is that doth go with thee; he will not fail thee, nor forsake thee.

—Deuteronomy 31:6

Sometimes God Presents Us with a Gift

Sometimes God presents us with a gift, but we are afraid to untie the ribbons and open it to see what is inside. I sit and stare at it, wondering whether to open it or lay it aside. *What if its contents are alive*, I ask? Will it jump out and scream at me in surprise? Or will it shrink away in fear of my face? How can I receive God's blessing in this gift from on high if I do not have courage to look inside? Perhaps its contents are a thing of beauty, a rare prize. I turn it round and round, looking at it upside down. I should not be so scared. It's just a box. What harm can there be? A little courage and belief that my Father in heaven cares deeply for me are all I need. Fill me with courage, O Lord, to believe in something far greater than me. God, it is You I need to see. Heaven is my destiny. Amen.

Be of good courage, and he shall strengthen your heart, all ye that hope in the LORD.

—Psalm 31:24

The Spirit of the Lord is upon me, because he hath anointed me to preach the gospel to the poor; he hath sent me to heal the brokenhearted, to preach deliverance to the captives, and recovering of sight to the blind, to set at liberty them that are bruised.

—Luke 4:18

Your Infinite Mercy Never Ceases to Amaze Me

O God, take away the pain wrought by evil that debilitates and diminishes countenance, creating despondency and despair that purge my heart of joy and peace. I will rejoice in You, O God, that You will deliver me from pain, enrapturing my heart with goodness and mercy. No longer do I need to hurt since You are here to heal my heart of past histories and defeats. It is by Your power that my bruised spirit is relieved and rejuvenated as darkness dissipates and evaporates into Your light. How marvelous, how wonderful a God You are. Your infinite mercy never ceases to amaze me. Amen.

Let us therefore come boldly unto the throne of grace, that we may obtain mercy, and find grace to help in time of need.

—Hebrews 4:16

And Jesus answering saith unto them, Have faith in God.

—Luke 17:5

And the apostles said unto the Lord, Increase our faith.

—Mark 11:22

Increase My Faith, O Lord

Through the remnant of your people, a scarlet thread was hidden among royal purple prepared for weaving. It was a thread so fine that it could not be seen by the naked eye. It is known only to those who have ears that have heard and eyes that have seen. The thread, stained with the blood of a lamb, weaves a fine tapestry of a kingdom not of this world but of a kingdom dreamed. What the eyes cannot see, and the ears cannot hear calls upon spirits of faith and belief. Increase my faith, O Lord, that I do not question what You enter into my heart, trusting You as nimble fingers stitch together the cloth of atonement held together by the scarlet thread. Faith is belief in You, O God—an intangible force evidenced by goodness and mercy. Help me remember that You are the Creator and I the created. Therefore, You deserve my declaration and exhortation of You as God Almighty. Amen.

Now faith is the substance of things hoped for, the evidence of things not seen.

—Hebrews 11:1

Being justified freely by his grace through the redemption that is in Christ Jesus:

Whom God hath set forth to be a propitiation through faith in his blood, to declare his righteousness for the remission of sins that are past, through the forbearance of God;

To declare, I say, at this time his righteousness: that he might be just, and the justifier of him which believeth in Jesus.

—Romans 3:24–26

My Spirit Is Quiet in Your Grace

My heart is pure and yet impure. I speak in words of anger. I am bitter and unforgiving. I commit to do Your will, but I am lazy and slothful. I am disobedient. I hear the Spirit, and yet I do not listen. I receive Your love and still do not believe. Your Spirit reveals, and yet I question. Time stands still in Your presence, and still I do not know You. I know what I know, and yet I sin in my flesh. My heart screams for deliverance. I seek Your touch. Your love flows through me. You cleanse my heart through tears of love. Your Spirit falls on me. Your blood covers me. You give me peace that passes all understanding and joy unspeakable. My spirit is quiet in your grace. Amen.

And he said unto me, My grace is sufficient for thee: for my strength is made perfect in weakness. Most gladly therefore will I rather glory in my infirmities, that the power of Christ may rest upon me.

—2 Corinthians 12:9

And it shall come to pass in the day that the LORD shall
give thee rest from thy sorrow, and from thy fear, and
from the hard bondage wherein thou wast made to serve.
                                                            —Isaiah 14:3

My Heart Healed of Sorrow; There Are No Tears

Sorrow and pain have been my companions most of my life, but I have no regrets. The lessons they have taught me illuminate my future. Mistakes were choices I made without asking You, Lord, for advice, but I have no regrets. My future is bright for having made them. If I had been willing to listen to Your voice for wisdom and guidance, perhaps I would not have bumped so hard; perhaps there would have been fewer tears. I have no regrets. For a while I was a box, and then it broke itself into a line that circled and became a sphere. Eventually, it cornered and stretched itself in three directions, pointing to choices of right and wrong, but I have no regrets. The path is straight before me. You, my future, stand before me in all Your glory. Blind eyes have been opened; closed ears can now hear. My heart has been healed of sorrow; there are no tears. My life is constantly changing as in a kaleidoscope of bits and pieces of colored glass ever transforming into prisms, each more beautiful than the last. Just when I thought I was not ready, You changed me into something new. You took me to places I did not want to go and kept me there while You broke the mold. Amen.

And God shall wipe away all tears from their eyes;
and there shall be no more death, neither sorrow,
nor crying, neither shall there be any more pain: for
the former things are passed away.
                                                            —Revelation 21:4

Roses among Thorns

Servants called to walk among roses and thorns,
abiding in belief, faith, trust, reform,
Endless quest to touch, reveal, transform,
those hearts pricked with poison from the thorns,
Hearts filled with loneliness, grief, and fear,
hearts that weep and mourn.

Sorrow and grief on every hand,
destitution reaching into every corner of the earth,
Servants' eyes see desolation, the ears hear cries,
as hands reach out to salvage damaged lives,
Bodies diseased, broken, and scarred search for strength
through eyes of anguish and empty hearts,
People powerless to rise above the stench of death,
no future, no hope, they cry for deliverance.

From the poem "The Resting Place"
by M. Kathryn Gray

The LORD hath called me from the womb; from the bowels of my mother hath he made mention of my name. And he hath made my mouth like a sharp sword; in the shadow of his hand hath he hid me, and made me a polished shaft; in his quiver hath he hid me.

—Isaiah 49:1–2

You Knew How Difficult the Task, the Call That You Asked

Father, believing that You have called me into service, believing the truth of Your Word, I move by Your power and Your grace. I do Thy will and not my own. Thanking You for Your faith in me, I ask for revelation, knowledge, and strength to do those things You have called me to do. You knew how difficult the task—the call that You asked. My time and talents belong to You. You must come first. No matter how great the sacrifice, it can never equal Yours. Struggle as I will, not my will but Thy will be done. Each day I do battle, the struggle goes on, but I will never go back. As Your servant, Lord, I will never return to a meaningless world of lust and pride. I will seek to live in a spiritual realm of humbleness far above the maddening crowds of flesh-eaters so I may be enabled to help them discover the depth of Your love for them. Amen.

And now, saith the LORD that formed me from the womb to be his servant . . . yet shall I be glorious in the eyes of the LORD, and my God shall be my strength.

—Isaiah 49:5

And God said, Let there be light: and there was light. And God saw the light, that it was good.
—Genesis 1:3–4

God, Fill Me with the Good Light

God, fill me with the good light that I will shine brilliantly for You. Make me a light unto the world that shines all the year through. Create in me Your light of power—Jesus in heart and deed—that I may give to all those willing to receive it. God, let Your light shine through me, blinding this world to the evil that creates chaos, darkness, and debris in the lives of Your children who are lost and lonely. May Your countenance that resides within me be a light upon the path that leads the way to salvation, love imparted, abounding in mercy and grace. Father, use me to break through hardened hearts that are broken and bound by chains attached to walls in the darkness of diverse places. The sound of Your name, Lord, exudes expectation that fulfills dreams and heals body, mind, and soul. It's the good light that shuts out darkness, revealing Your greatness, Your lovingkindness, Your soul. Amen.

To give light to them that sit in darkness and in the shadow of death, to guide our feet into the way of peace.
—Luke 1:79

*If thy whole body therefore be full of light, having no
part dark, the whole shall be full of light, as when
the bright shining of a candle doth give thee light.*
—Luke 11:36

Dear God, If You Would Help Me Light Just One Little Candle

Your people, Father, are wrapped in cloaks of self-centeredness, hiding Your righteousness in dark chambers behind prison walls. Bound by chains of deceit, their hearts rot and decay in cold, empty places with no boundaries, a void that seems impossible to cross. The darkness is more black than any black known to mankind—thick, almost impenetrable, permeated with demons of pride, lust, hatred, and sin. Dear God, if You would help me light just one little candle that would illuminate the dark, I could help the world see the light that You are. Just one tiny spark, and the touch of Your breath will awaken a sleeping heart. With just one small spark, You can set the captive free to ignite the world with warmth that comes only from Your light. Use me as Your instrument from which Your love may be seen that You and I together can set the world on fire that all people should be free! Amen.

*For thou wilt light my candle: the LORD my God
will enlighten my darkness.*
—Psalm 18:28

*I will praise the LORD according to his righteousness:
and will sing praise to the name of the LORD most
high.*

—Psalm 7:17

Giver of Light and Righteousness

I come before You, Father, to praise You. You are the Word.
You are the Alpha and Omega, the Bright and Morning Star,
the giver of light and righteousness, the author of faith, the
redeemer of sin, the deliverer of bondage. You are my anchor
in a sea of turmoil. It is by You and through You that all things
are made possible. My eyes are lifted up to You. I love You,
Father, above all other. I bow before You; I worship and adore
You. I thank You for this gift so rare—Your love, Your Spirit,
jewels beyond compare. The trumpets of my heart proclaim
Your name to the world. Bells ring, angels sing, and I dance to
You, my Lord. All creation in heaven and on earth sing praises
to the all-powerful and exalted above all—the Father, Son, and
Holy Ghost! Amen.

*I will be glad and rejoice in thee: I will sing praise to
thy name, O thou most High.*

—Psalm 9:2

Though he were a Son, yet learned, He obedience by the things which he suffered; And being made perfect, he became the author of eternal salvation unto all them that obey Him.

—Hebrews 5:8–9

Not My Will, but Thy Will

It is very early morning, and the world about me is in darkness, waiting for the first rays of sunlight to fill the heavens. The earth beneath me rotates toward the light of the sun, revealing the expanse of God's heavens above. It is quiet except for the tinkling of the chimes in the gentle breeze. Stars dot the heavens in the deep blue of the night. Tranquility overshadows all fear and brings peace beyond understanding. It is just you and I, God. I listen for His voice. "Not my will, but thy will," my heart says to Him. It is just God and I, my heart listening to hear His desires for my life. "Go and sell that which you have, and buy the field that holds the treasure of the Most High God," I hear Him say. "Uncover the secrets that lay beneath the surface above all the world can offer. Wear them as jewels about your neck, adorned as a queen for her king." The essence of life glitters and shines as the treasure is opened, the brilliance of God bursting forth, the essence of the Holy Spirit, a most rare fragrance unlike any found on earth. It's the kingdom at hand that consumes all other purposes for existing in a mundane world of children of the Most High God who have ears that do not hear and eyes that do not see the truth of

Your omnipresence and expansiveness. You are Alpha and Omega, King of kings, Lord of lords, ruler of the universe. Thank you, Father, for this truth. Thank you for Your guiding light. Thank you for anointing me and using me as Your vessel to pour new wine into the lives of others. Amen.

> *For as by one man's disobedience many were made sinners, so by the obedience of one shall many be made righteous.*
> —Romans 5:19

But he giveth more grace. Wherefore he saith, God resisteth the proud, but giveth grace unto the humble. Humble yourselves in the sight of the Lord, and he shall lift you up.

—James 4:6,10

Cleanse My Heart, and Keep Me Humble

O Father, as I walk in Your stead, following in Your footsteps, do not let me falter and receive a spirit of superiority. Cleanse my heart, and keep me humble that I may be led by You, that I do not fall into evil, thinking I am greater than thou to my brothers and sisters. Bless me with the knowledge that my purpose is to draw them nigh unto You that they may receive Your Spirit and anointing to perpetuate the good news of the gospel. You and only You, God Almighty, deserve to be placed in the height of glory and I in lowliness of servitude. Amen.

For he that is called in the Lord, being a servant, is the Lord's freeman: likewise also he that is called, being free, is Christ's servant.

—1 Corinthians 7:22

For the Son of man is come to save that which was lost.
—Matthew 18:11

Souls Lost

Her sorrow is evident, her countenance low. Sad eyes look away quickly. Dear Jesus, it is the eyes that reveal the soul, tormented or peace aglow. I have watched as she works silently, going through motions with no purpose, sadness snuffing out any spark of joy. My heart cries for her, this girl with the purple hair. My prayer, dear God is for You to help me to help her. Let her see You, Jesus, through me. The tattoos on her body, the rings in her ears, and the purple hair cry out for someone to hear, "I'm lost. Please help me find the way to my father's house." Break me . . . mold me . . . use me, I pray. Touch me that I can touch her. Give me Your love that I can give it to her. Change me so You can change her. You said, "Even so it is not the will of your Father which is in heaven, that one of these little ones should perish" (Matthew 19:14). Dear Jesus, let us—You and I—save this little one. Amen.

> *What man of you, having an hundred sheep, if he lose one of them, doth not leave the ninety and nine in the wilderness, and go after that which is lost, until he finds it?*
>
> —Luke 15:4

I am the vine, ye are the branches: He that abideth in me, and I in him, the same bringeth forth much fruit: for without me ye can do nothing.

—John 15:5

That My Fruit Will Increase to Overflowing

The many years I have walked with You have increased my faith in Your plan for my life. I am lifted up with hope that my fruit will increase to overflowing. Thank You for Your discipline. And oh, the pruning—how it has hurt. But I have matured and am drawn closer to You. I look down the road on which I have walked—a long, winding road. I can see myself at the beginning. I have come so far, but I still have so far to go. Thank You for breaking me and molding me to Your will that I may abide in You. I walk toward You with increasing anticipation. I want to move to greater heights. I want more of You. I ask Your blessing to expand my territory that I should live in Your presence with abundant joy. Amen.

The fruit of the righteous is a tree of life; and he that winneth souls is wise.

—Proverbs 11:30

Abiding in God's Presence

Jesus, Jesus, you are mine,
You have lifted me to realms sublime.
The trumpets of my heart proclaim your name to the world!
Bells ring, angels sing, I dance to you, my Lord!

Everywhere I look you are only what I see.
Jesus, Jesus you are mine, I am yours,
And this gift, no one can ever take from me.

Gift of all gifts, priceless and pure,
Touching Spirit to spirit you reveal yourself to me,
In a magnificent realm of sublime and true ecstasy.

All-powerful and eminent exalted above all,
Creation in heaven and earth sing praises to Father,
Son, and Holy Ghost!

From the poem "Millennial Christmas"
by Mary Kathy Gray

And I say unto you, Ask, and it shall be given you; seek, and ye shall find; knock, and it shall be opened unto you.

—Luke 11:9

Behold, I Stand at the Door and Knock

O Lord, my God, how lovely is Thy countenance. In the wee hours of the morning, You have bid me awake with the sweet smell of Thy perfume filling my nostrils with the delight of Your presence. The aura of Thy light shines forth into my heart, illuminating darkness. I knocked, and You opened the door. I asked, and You gave me what I asked for. Spirits of dread and fear are driven into darkness by the spirit of hope. You knocked, and I opened unto You. Peace was at the door. Confidence resides here. Amen.

Behold, I stand at the door, and knock: if any man hear my voice, and open the door, I will come in to him, and will sup with him, and he with me.

—Revelation 3:20

I indeed baptize you with water unto repentance:
but he that cometh after me is mightier than I,
whose shoes I am not worthy to bear: he shall baptize
you with the Holy Ghost, and with fire.

—Matthew 3:11

I Am Consumed with You, O God

God in His magnificent glory supplies all my needs. His desires are my desires. His countenance fills the atmosphere about me. He breathes; I breathe. He laughs; I laugh. He cries; I cry. His thoughts are my thoughts. His words are my words. As I write, I am one with Him. I am consumed with You, O God. My heart is a fire burning to light the paths of those who are walking astray into the wilderness of sin, athirst for righteousness and truth. To be consumed by You, there is nothing else, and I love that which *is*. As I listen in the solitude of this moment, You speak, and I know that You are God. Amen.

Whose fan is in his hand, and he will thoroughly
purge his floor, and gather his wheat into the garner;
but he will burn up the chaff with unquenchable fire.

—Matthew 3:12

And a very great multitude spread their garments in the way; others cut down branches from the trees, and strawed them in the way.
—Matthew 21:8

God, I Have Chosen You

God, I have chosen You above all others. You are the priority of my life. You are the Word. You are the beginning and the end. You were *before* the foundation of the world. You are God, and I have chosen You to reside in my heart. You are sacred in my heart with love for You that only You could give me. You comfort me by Your Holy Spirit. I choose to live Your Word and believe that You are real. Those I love have said that I am overzealous and fanatical because I have chosen to take all of You into my heart. I cry out in anguish against indifference to You. I am saddened by the world's complacency and denial of Your reality. My heart screams out against stubborn traditions that dull the senses and harden the heart. Blood trickles from my heart each time tradition steals Your identity. I am wounded with each mockery of Your sacrifice. I walk before You, laying palms at your feet and shouting, "Hail, King Jesus," giver of light and righteousness, author of faith, redeemer of sin, deliverer of bondage and anchor in a sea of turmoil. As each new day dawns, I, a soldier of the cross, march forward. Because I have chosen You, I can forgive and love all the more with a heart of compassion only You can give for those who are blinded and cannot see, for those who deny Your majesty. Amen.

And the multitudes that went before, and that followed, cried, saying, Hosanna to the son of David: Blessed is he that cometh in the name of the Lord; Hosanna in the highest.
—Matthew 21:9

He shall not be afraid of evil tidings: his heart is fixed, trusting in the LORD.
—Psalm 112:7

Direct My Heart, O God

Direct my heart, O God, that my focus should remain fixed on You. Let the supplication of my heart forever be praises unto Thee. In the quiet darkness, let the thoughts of my heart drift toward You like a piece of wood floating in a sea to an unknown destination. I, a piece of driftwood, bobbing up and down, floating in the sea of life, search for answers to unasked questions that You, God, already know the answers to before the questions are formed in my mind. Hidden currents, one often stronger than another, pull me away from You, and yet I still move forward to my ultimate destination. Sometimes I am completely overpowered by hidden currents that may pull me under dark waters, but as I continually move toward You, O God, I resurface, glistening in the sun. Outer extremities have been changed as pieces of frail, dead wood have broken off in the strength of the current, as rough edges have been smoothed into soft, rounded, sharp edges until I come to rest on the sandy beaches of humbleness. Let my spirit be drawn into the purity of You, like white, sandy beaches made clean from crystal blue waters washing away impurities, taking them away into unseen depths of a bottomless abyss. As the shade of tall palms swaying in the breeze cool the sands beneath them, I am drawn to You, seeking divine absolution for my life. Amen.

My heart is fixed, O God, my heart is fixed: I will sing and give praise.
—Psalm 57:7

If any of you lack wisdom, let him ask of God, that giveth to all men liberally, and upbraideth not; and it shall be given him.

—James 1:5

Help Me, O Lord, to Know Wisdom

Wisdom speaks to the inner spirit. It knows no boundaries. It is what directs you to paths of righteousness. Wisdom is another name of the Holy Spirit. Wisdom is He that imparts knowledge and defines your direction, stabilizes your energy, and sets straight your thoughts. Wisdom is a gift from God manifested through the Holy Spirit. Wisdom is the Holy Spirit. As rainwater pours over a mountain, it seeks to reach the highest point of its lowest level so it can pool into a reservoir containing itself for perpetual use. Help me, O Lord, to know Wisdom. Help me to recognize when He speaks, revealing righteous choice. My life is defined by the pouring out of living waters bubbling up and overflowing into rivers seeking the highest points of the lowest levels, filling pools that nourish multitudes with the fluid of everlasting life. As I receive Wisdom, so I receive the Holy Spirit. It is with Wisdom that I receive wisdom. Amen.

And Joshua the son of Nun was full of the spirit of wisdom; for Moses had laid his hands upon him: and the children of Israel hearkened unto him, and did as the LORD commanded Moses.

—Deuteronomy 34:9

Wait on the LORD: be of good courage, and he shall strengthen thine heart: wait, I say, on the LORD.

—Psalm 27:14

Waiting upon the Lord

Father, You have given me knowledge that I should remember the days of old, kings of evil leading people in disobedience born of impatience and reared by lust, and people failing You time and time again. Ignorant of wisdom and belief in Your sovereignty, restless souls sought to please themselves. If only they had remembered Jabez's cry for mercy and protection. Wanderers in perverse lands, they looked to themselves to fulfill need and desire, ignoring your messengers who were delivering instructions that would change their lives in monumental proportions. Ignorant and impatient, leaning to their own understanding, they forfeited wisdom, choosing to worship idols of cold, dead clay. I ask You, Lord, to give me patience that I will wait for Your answers for my life, that I will grow in wisdom as I discern evil, rebuke every unclean thing, hear Your voice, and trust in the words You put in my heart. Teach me to wait. It is well with You that Your children trust and walk by faith in the knowledge that Your plan for individual lives are part of the scheme of Your greater plan for Your kingdom. It is through waiting that I move by process ever closer to You. As a salmon waiting patiently for the right moment to thrust forward and upward against strong waters, rising a little higher with each effort, so I rise to reach a level with You that spawns growth from the power of Your presence. For this reason, I will wait upon You, O God. Amen.

> *But they that wait upon the LORD shall renew their strength; they shall mount up with wings as eagles; they shall run, and not be weary; and they shall walk, and not faint.*
>
> —Isaiah 40:31

The LORD is my strength and song, and he is become my salvation: he is my God, and I will prepare him an habitation; my father's God, and I will exalt him.

—Exodus 15:2

Stay with Me, Lord; Thy Strength Is My Strength

O Lord, my God, open my eyes to truth that my heart may be filled with Your presence. Fill me with Your Spirit, Lord, that I may be made strong and righteous unto You. My soul longs to be in Your presence that I should know Your power and glorify You in it. It is by Your strength that I am made whole in my weakness. I am lifted upright when I hear You whisper my name telling, me to arise and walk as You lead me on a journey that strengthens my faith and guides me toward heavenly dominion. Stay with me, Lord. Thy strength is my strength. Amen.

I know thy works: behold, I have set before thee an open door, and no man can shut it: for thou hast a little strength, and hast kept my word, and hast not denied my name.

—Revelation 3:8

For we which have believed do enter into rest, as he said, As I have sworn in my wrath, if they shall enter into my rest: although the works were finished from the foundation of the world.

—Hebrews 4:3

Resting Quietly in the Lord

I sit in complete peace, my mind resting quietly in the Lord. I am surrounded by a world full of itself, selfishness, and greed with lonely faces seeking unknown peace, weary from coming to and fro seeking whom they may devour. But, I, having found the Lord, sit unobstructed in peace, my heart full of joy, knowing that life everlasting awaits me when I go to that place of beauty, bountiful with love. I raise my glass of new wine and drink with the King of all kings in His heaven divine. I cannot wait until the morrow. Each day is afresh with uncommon relief from love renewed. Sorrows behind, joy comes in the morning. Fresh, clean water flowing into and bubbling forth from my spirit, life is perpetually renewed. Amen.

Peace I leave with you, my peace I give unto you: not as the world giveth, give I unto you. Let not your heart be troubled, neither let it be afraid.

—John 14:27

Daily Journey

I met a man called Jesus who knows all about me,
From the least to the most, from the worst to be best
From the start.

He speaks my name, He calls me out,
To proclaim his love, his mercy, his healing, his name!
This man called Jesus fills me with power to destroy Satan's gain.

His life – my life, one in the same.

From the poem "I Met a Man Called Jesus"
by Mary Kathy Gray

My soul is weary of my life; I will leave my complaint
upon myself; I will speak in the bitterness of my soul.
—Job 10:1

Help Me, O Lord, to Define My Priorities

Life gets so boring sometimes, Lord, with my daily same-ole, same-ole routine—get up early, go to bed late. Lord, I'm tired. I just want to lie down and die so I can get some rest. My nose to the grindstone, I push, push, push. Round and round I go to keep up the pace. On a roller coaster ride up and down—will it ever end?—dipping into depths that take my breath away and choke me of my very life. This is not what You intended for my life. How did I get to this place of stress and distress? Peace is what I long for, time to spend with You. I open my Bible to read, and the telephone rings. I kneel to pray, and someone knocks on the door. I pick up an inspired book, read it halfway through, and then there is an interruption. God, how can I get to You? How can I become a vessel to pour out new wine if nothing flows in? Help me, O Lord, to define my priorities and put You first place upon the altar of my heart so I can grow in wisdom and knowledge. Help me to be patient with the tasks set before me. Help me to see the truth of the moment and act in obedience to Your voice. Maneuver my footsteps along the path You would have me trod, walking in your light toward "the high calling of God in Christ Jesus" (Philippians 3:14) that I should reach my destiny in You. Amen.

But they that wait upon the LORD shall renew their
strength; they shall mount up with wings as eagles;
they shall run, and not be weary; and they shall
walk, and not faint.
—Isaiah 40:31

Behold, the LORD thy God hath set the land before thee: go up and possess it, as the LORD God of thy fathers hath said unto thee; fear not, neither be discouraged.

—Deuteronomy 1:21

Help Me, O Lord, when I Am Discouraged

Help me, O Lord, when I am discouraged. Help me to remember that Thy ways are not my ways. Help me to believe and know that You are in everything and that Your timing is perfect. The sum total of my life is in the outcome of what You and You alone have knowledge of. The orchestration of my life is in Your hands, the melody being played by skilled fingers as on a fine harp. I wanted this or that, but You said, "No, that is too easy." I wanted this or that, but You said, "Now is not the time." I expected the harvest now, but You said, "I must wait for rain." So what if *this* or *that* does not happen? Help me understand that it does not mean You have forsaken me but that You have commanded me saying, "Trust in the LORD with all thine heart; and lean not unto thine own understanding" (Prov. 3:5). Let my joy overflow unto You, O God, that I am assured of what I cannot see and have no knowledge of what is written in Your heart to be revealed in the day of Thy choosing. Amen.

Be strong and of a good courage, fear not, nor be afraid of them: for the LORD thy God, he it is that doth go with thee; he will not fail thee, nor forsake thee.

—Deuteronomy 31:6

PRAYERS

*And I will come down and talk with thee there:
and I will take of the spirit which is upon thee,
and will put it upon them; and they shall bear the
burden of the people with thee, that thou bear it
not thyself alone.*

—Numbers 11:17

Flesh against Spirit

Father, forgive me for being so weak that I cannot stand alone.
My flesh cries out; my spirit says no! I rejoice in my trials, but
my heart fills with fear. Needs and lusts of the flesh overwhelm
me. Help me, O Lord; set me free. So small and inept,
overshadowed with pride, overcome with sorrow, I struggle
flesh against spirit, all hope hidden behind the veil. You, too,
have known the pain of separation; how great the hurt. My soul
cries "go;" my spirit says "stay." But wait! There is a brighter day!
Be happy with where I am, for joy comes in the morning. I am
alone and lonely yet never alone. Your love floods over me, and
joy fills my heart. My tears are not for me; I shed them for You.
What purpose are tears but to know You, my God. Oh, how
I love You. New miracles are born each day. Peace comes, and
once again I walk unafraid and never alone. Amen.

*Beloved, think it not strange concerning the fiery
trial which is to try you, as though some strange
thing happened unto you: But rejoice, inasmuch as
ye are partakers of Christ's sufferings; that, when
his glory shall be revealed, ye may be glad also with
exceeding joy.*

—1 Peter 4:12–13

In God have I put my trust: I will not be afraid what man can do unto me.

—Psalm 56:11

Teach Me, O God, Not to Worry

Teach me, O God, not to worry. When I worry, it becomes evident that I do not trust You. If I believe that You care intimately for everything about me, then I should not concern myself with *any* aspect of life. The baggage of life that weights down my spirit dictates that I should lean to my own understanding. Deliver me from the spirit of rebellion that entices me to ignore Your authority and ability to absolve all issues without my help that in actuality are under Your control. Deception leads me to sin against You. Forgive me, Father, for failing to relinquish control to You. Remind me to wait for Your answers. Teach me, O God, not to worry that I may live a life of peace without worry. Amen.

Fear thou not; for I am with thee: be not dismayed; for I am thy God: I will strengthen thee; yea, I will help thee; yea, I will uphold thee with the right hand of my righteousness.

—Isaiah 41:10

Yea, forty years didst thou sustain them in the wilderness, so that they lacked nothing; their clothes waxed not old, and their feet swelled not.
—Nehemiah 9:21

No Need to Fear; I Am in the Palm of Your Hand

It is in silence that I hear Your voice. In perfect stillness, not even the air moves. I close my eyes and wait. Your presence grows stronger. Then Your words come. I am filled with new knowledge, nourishment to sustain Your Spirit that dwells within my soul, hungry for substance of truth and thirsty for righteousness. My heart refreshed; I am reassured of Your everlasting provision for me. There is no need to fear; I am in the palm of Your hand. The earth does not matter nor anything in it. You remind me, "Heaven and earth shall pass away, but my words shall not pass away" (Matthew 24:35). It is in the Spirit that I have come to this place, and in the Spirit I will return unto You that we will become one. All heaven will rejoice in this reunion. Amen.

Cast thy burden upon the LORD, and he shall sustain thee: he shall never suffer the righteous to be moved.
—Psalm 55:22

Let us therefore come boldly unto the throne of grace, that we may obtain mercy, and find grace to help in time of need.

—Hebrews 4:16

Father, Help Me

Father, help me look deeper to understand my spouse's needs. Help me respond sincerely and be the companion I was meant to be. Show me how to appreciate the relationship more. Help me appreciate my grown children. Help me remember how I felt at their age. May I not interfere, pass judgment, or criticize. Help me love my friends and coworkers, realizing and expecting their need of me. Help me be tolerant when they invade my space with frivolity. Help me to be a blessing to them and an instrument of Your peace.

Father, help me receive strangers and give them the benefit of the doubt, assuming no evil. Help me to spiritually uplift and encourage those who come to my door in the name of Jesus with my interest at heart. Help me to be tolerant and understanding, for I may be entertaining Your angels unaware. Help me accept my responsibility of personifying You and fulfill Your desires for my life. Father, help me. Amen.

But be not thou far from me, O LORD: O my strength, haste thee to help me.

—Psalm 22:19

But I say unto you, Love your enemies, bless them that curse you, do good to them that hate you and pray for them which despitefully use you, and persecute you; That ye may be the children of your Father which is in heaven: for he maketh his sun to rise on the evil and on the good, and sendeth rain on the just and on the unjust.

—Matthew 5:44–45

Through You, O God, I Can Love Unconditionally

God has set my heart free as His love flows through me—no anger, no hatred, no bitterness. Rudeness directed at me is of no consequence. Lies told of me cannot hinder the outpouring of love to those who offend me. When blame rears its ugly head in misguided assault, I stand ready to retaliate with forgiveness. Snide remarks I hear; words coming out of mouths of evil cannot harm me. Because those who speak have not love and have not discovered who they are in Christ, I forgive them of the evil that binds them to hell. I do not need their approval of who I am. I am who I am. God made me who I am, and when they reject me, they reject Him. What does it matter what they say or how they behave? It is only important that they remember the love that flows through me to them—God's *unconditional* love. Through You, O God, I can love unconditionally. Amen.

But love ye your enemies, and do good, and lend, hoping for nothing again; and your reward shall be great, and ye shall be the children of the Highest: for he is kind unto the unthankful and to the evil. Be ye therefore merciful, as your Father also is merciful. Judge not, and ye shall not be judged: condemn not, and ye shall not be condemned: forgive, and ye shall be forgiven.

—Luke 6:35–37

EPILOGUE

I believe these prayers are writings inspired by God to help you become aware of and alert to the power of intimate communion with God. As you have turned these pages, I pray that you have used the first person—I, me, my—because this was written for you. Allow yourself to become vulnerable to God, and allow Him to transport you to a plane high above the world.

Stop being a tough guy or a stealth lady. Get on your knees, or lie prostrate on the floor. Bend to His will. Allow Him to release your sin. Cry the tears. Show Him how much you want Him and need Him. Talk to Him. Let it go! Fear not. "I am with you always, even unto the end of the world" (Matthew 28:20).

QUICK REFERENCES

The Cross

- » Father, Give Me Strength to Make the Right Choice (Choice)
- » Amazing Love (Christ's Sacrifice)
- » That I Should Be Changed and Born Again (New Birth)
- » Bring Me Home (Deliverance)
- » Unless I Die Daily to Self, I Cannot Know You, O Lord (Repentance)
- » Chastise Me, O God, That My Spirit May Be Stripped of Pride (Cleansing)
- » My Desire Is to Serve You, O Lord (Desire)
- » Direct Me, O Lord, That I May Follow Your Lead to My Destiny (Destiny)

Joy in the Morning

- » Deliver Me, O God, while There Is Still Time to Save Me (Battle)
- » Lord, Help Me to Identify the Evil That Pervades My Spirit (Discernment)
- » The Power of Pain Exalts You, O Lord (Deliverance)
- » Sometimes God Presents Us with a Gift (Courage)
- » Your Infinite Mercy Never Ceases to Amaze Me (Mercy)
- » Increase My Faith, O Lord (Faith)
- » My Spirit Is Quiet in Your Grace (Grace)
- » My Heart Healed of Sorrow, There Are No Tears (Healing)

Roses among Thorns
- » You Knew How Difficult the Task, the Call That You Asked (Servitude)
- » God, Fill Me with the Good Light (Love)
- » Dear God, If You Would Help Me Light Just One Little Candle (Help)
- » Giver of Light and Righteousness (Praise)
- » Not My Will, But Thy Will (Commitment)
- » Cleanse My Heart, and Keep Me Humble (Humbleness)
- » Souls Lost (Unsaved)
- » That My Fruit Will Increase to Overflowing (Fruitfulness)

Abiding in God's Presence
- » Behold, I Stand at the Door and Knock (God's Presence)
- » I Am Consumed with You, O God (Fire)
- » God, I Have Chosen You (Allegiance)
- » Direct My Heart, O God (Focus)
- » Help Me, O Lord, to Know Wisdom (Wisdom)
- » Waiting upon the Lord (Patience)
- » Stay with Me Lord, Thy Strength Is My Strength (Strength)
- » Resting Quietly in the Lord (Peace)

Daily Journey
- » I Am at Crossroads, Which Way Do I Go? (Decision)
- » Help Me, O Lord, to Define My Priorities (Weariness)
- » Help Me, O Lord, when I Am Discouraged (Discouragement)
- » Flesh against Spirit (Struggle)

- » O Lord, Teach Me Not to Worry (Peace)
- » No Need to Fear, I Am in the Palm of Your Hand (Provision)
- » Father, Help Me (Relationships)
- » Through You, O God, I Can Love Unconditionally (Forgiveness)

ABOUT THE AUTHOR

Mary Kathy Gray was born in Fort Worth, Texas. In 1969, Mary Kathy and her family moved to Arkansas where they operated a commercial poultry and cattle farm. Today, her sons, Larry and Michael live nearby her home in Dardanelle, Arkansas. In 2017, she became Mary Gray-Sand, marrying Duane Sand who has a son, David. She has two grandchildren, Aaryn and Derrick, and great grandchild, Aspen Dawn Gray. Mary Kathy was trained as a classical pianist while attending colleges in Texas and Arkansas. Today, her business career has led to helping older citizens with their Medicare Insurance as an Independent Agent.

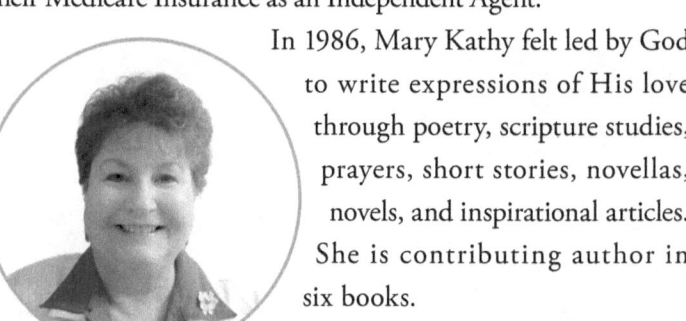

In 1986, Mary Kathy felt led by God to write expressions of His love through poetry, scripture studies, prayers, short stories, novellas, novels, and inspirational articles. She is contributing author in six books.

WHAT PEOPLE ARE SAYING ABOUT
THE CALL OF THE MOURNING DOVES

I f you desire a more meaningful prayer experience, *The Call of the Mourning Doves*, is for you. Mary Kathy has included prayers you can pray. God is concerned about our needs, but the relationship God desires with His children is more expansive. I agree with her when she wrote, "These prayers are to help you learn how to commune with the Lord on a spiritual plane that is above earthly rhetoric and self-reliance."

Mary Kathy Gray's book, *The Call of the Mourning Doves*, will expand your concept of prayer. Her own experience with her heavenly Father has opened revelatory truths about intimacy and communion with the triune God. This book will inspire and instruct you in your pursuit of a relationship with God.

ALTON GARRISON
CHAIRMAN CHURCH HEALTH COMMISSION
WORLD ASSEMBLIES OF GOD FELLOWSHIP
EXECUTIVE DIRECTOR OF ACTS 2 JOURNEY COHORT

www.ingramcontent.com/pod-product-compliance
Lightning Source LLC
Chambersburg PA
CBHW020803130626
46554CB00006B/2296